Python Made Simple

Full Beginner's Guide to Mastering Python

Project Syntax

Table of Contents

Legal notice

About this eBook

Do you feel that the world we live in has been so engulfed in artificial technology that it is getting to a point you can barely relate? Do you ever wish you were a part of those that actually contribute to the development of these technologies but they seems so complicated that you would not know where to start?

Well, congratulations on finding a starting point if you are a newbie to programing. There is no better way to start being a part of the solution (as opposed to being part of the ignorant masses) than by picking up this book and starting to learn to become a programmer.

At Project Syntax, we are on a mission to equip everyone with the ability to write in computer language to make the machines solve our problems with less difficulty. This Python guide adopts a learn-first, then-understand approach to show you the incredible power of Python. The best way to learn is to:

1. *Follow the guide step-by-step in its original chapter order.* You will carry out programming exercises to see how the code works, then you will learn why we type the code the way it is.

2. *You must pay attention to detail in every exercise.* What sets a good programmer apart from a lousy one is how attentive they are to every character, space, and symbol in the code.

3. *Make the code run and write your own code based on each example.* Use the pointers provided to create your own Python scripts or go online to such sites as *StackOverflow* or *CodeFights* to practice and expand on what you have learned.

Rinse and repeat for the next exercise. Remember, the key to progressive learning is *consistency* and *persistence*.

This eBook imparts all the essential skills and knowledge that a beginner programmer must master to become a proficient programmer. If you follow its instructions to the latter and still you get errors or get the results you are not expecting, go back to the beginning of the exercise and study your code in detail, not just throw in the towel. You must have an eye for detail to be able to detect the tiniest bugs in your code.

Who this ebook is For

The Full Beginner's Guide to Mastering Python trains you by demonstrating what is happening and explaining it so you are able to replicate it in another exercise, rather than just telling you how to do something. If you have the desire to be the best Python programmer you can be, this book is for you. If you have already learned to write computer programs in other languages – be it a simple language like HTML5 or a more complex high-level language like C# – then this book is for you.

This book teaches the concepts and syntax of the Python programming language and requires that each exercise be typed in a text editor manually. We strive to simplify the learning process for those who buy our book, and as such, we also offer practice files for all the exercises in the .py format to help you compare what you do with what to expect.

If you have basic computer skills, some time to study (preferably one to two hours a day), and a good internet connection, then you have all it takes to make the most of this eBook. This is a stepping stone to a future where you get to choose the path that involves using the skills you learn now to instruct a computer how to solve your problems.

About Project Syntax

The future of humanity is defined by the code we write now. That is what we at Project Syntax believe. Our organization was founded on the desire to produce high quality yet simply illustrated and concise learning materials that will help beginners enter into the world of programming by 'learning through attempting first'. The Full Beginner's Guide to Mastering Python eBook is one of the materials that our dedicated team of experienced researchers and programmers have created to train complete beginners like you on the art of writing code.

Whether you are a complete newbie to programming or have experience writing code in some other language and wish to learn Python to expand it, you have chosen the right book. We believe that most learning instructions on the internet and in published books do not use the right approach, which is to show the learner how to do it first, and after they grasp the how, explain the why.

Project Syntax is passionate about teaching the public to write code. We believe that in time, everyone will be able to contribute towards the future of humanity by learning to write computer programs. Besides the Full Beginner's Guide to Mastering Python, we also have another eBook title "Full Beginner's Guide to Mastering Hacking" in the pipeline.

Feedback and Questions

We always welcome all forms of feedback from our readers – compliments, complaints, corrections, and questions – regarding the content of our eBooks. We would like to know what you think about this book, what you like and what you do not, as well as what you found useful and what you did not.

Your feedback is important because it helps us create titles that will best help you and others learn the coding and hacking skills they seek fast and with less difficulty.

Do not hesitate to contact us if you have something to say.

Chapter 1: Introduction to Python

Python is a high level programming language.

A programming language is how a computer programmer can issue instructions for the computer to follow when solving a problem.

Python was named after the Monty Python Flying Circus comedy group that was popular in the UK between 1969 and 1974.

There are tens if not hundreds of programming languages in use today, and they all are different in many ways. Python has grown to be one of the most popular for many reasons. Top among them is that it is a very powerful language that powers the algorithms of some of the biggest global companies such as Google and Yahoo, and top global websites including Reddit.

Despite this, Python is a language that is very easy to learn. Learning to become a programmer is not as hard as it used to be; in fact, you will find it fun and very engaging.

The best part about learning to write computer programs with the Python language is that compared to other object-oriented programming languages in use today such as C, C++, C#, and Java, Python was designed not just for the end result, but also to make the process of writing code an adventure on its own. There are 20 core principles that influenced the design and creation of the Python Programming Language, dubbed the Zen of Python, 19 of which are written down. Here are the first 10 principles of Python to help you appreciate why the language was made the way it is:

1. Beautiful is better than ugly.
2. Explicit is better than implicit.
3. Simple is better than complex.
4. Complex is better than complicated.
5. Flat is better than nested.
6. Sparse is better than dense.

7.   Readability counts.

8.   Special cases are not special enough to break the rules.

9.   Practicality beats purity.

10.   Errors should never pass silently.

While this eBook will not magically transform you into a a badass programmer ready to make the big bucks, it is an excellent stepping stone whether you want to pursue computer programming to expand your career, to start a new one, or just to know how to build your own programs.

Considering that 'fun' is a great motivator, every effort has been taken to make the process of learning using this book engaging and enjoyable for all users -- from first-time programmers to seasoned developers looking to add Python to their belt of programming languages they have mastered.

As you join the hundreds of thousands of other learners striving to master Python, the best word of advice I can leave you with is this one great quote:

"In many ways, (Python) is a dull language, borrowing solid old concepts and styles from many other languages: boring syntax, unsurprising semantics, few automatic coercions, etc. But that's one of the things I like about Python."

- *Tim Peters*

Why Python?

If you did your research well before choosing to buy this eBook, you probably discovered that Python is by far the most studied and the most widely used high-level programming language today. This is not just because it emphasizes on code readability and simple syntax, or because it requires fewer lines of code to create a program compared to other languages; here are the top seven reasons why you should see your decision to take on Python programming studies to the end:

1 Python opens up endless opportunities for programmers

Python developers are making a killing freelancing and taking up permanent jobs because the language is very popular among companies and organizations. Once you get comfortable with coding sing Python, you will be in a good position to consider job opportunities and even gigs that pay you to apply the concepts you learn in this book.

2. Python is a preferred language for web development

The number of websites on the World Wide Web is approaching the 1 billion mark and one facet of this evolution is the growing scope of Python in web development. Python brings a lot of flexibility and an array of ready-to-use framework (such as django, Zope2, Pylons, Grok, and web.py) that are revolutionizing how the front and back end of websites are built. Learning to create websites in Python is the best way to position yourself on the right side of history.

3. Learning computational thinking with Python is easy

Python is a high-level programming language that reads like regular English. Because of this, many English-speaking learners find it very easy to understand its syntax and how to use the various components of the language with minimal complexity. If you are a beginner, you will be surprised how easy it is to tell the computer what to do in Python and to think in ways that helps you conceptualize computer code.

4. Python has a rich and vibrant online community

As you enter the world of programming, you will discover soon enough how important the developer community is to the language and to its learners. The Python community is the 5th largest on *StackOverflow* community and the fourth most used language on *Github*. When you venture to the cyberspace to interact with other learners and with professionals, you will be taken aback by the huge number of people ready to help you learn by answering your questions and checking your code.

5. Python has one of the most mature package libraries

Most programming, as you will discover soon, is repetitive. When you start writing code on a commercial scale, you will appreciate the fact that Python is backed by repositories such as PyPI with hundreds of thousands of free modules and scripts that you can grab and use in your code. These modules and scripts bring pre-packaged functionality to your Python environment to solve a myriad of problems that you would otherwise have to deal with one-by-one. With Python, there is no need to re-invent the wheel.

6. Python is cross-platform and open source

Python has been around for over 20 years and throughout that period, it has been developed as a cross-platform and open source software that runs on Linux, Windows, and MacOS. Besides, the language is backed by over 2 decades of kink-straightening and bug-squashing which has turned it into a power house that makes your code run like you intended it on whichever platform.

7. Learning Python is the ideal stepping stone to other languages

There aren't many languages today that offer the simplicity and versatility of Python, but different people choose their languages of specialty for their own reasons. Even if you intend to specialize in some other high-level programming language e.g. C#, C++, or Java, Python is a great language to learn first before diversifying into another language.

Installing Python

In order to begin writing Python scripts and execute them on your computer, you must first set up the right software on your computer. Nothing is complicated at this stage, just as long as you follow the right steps. If you already know how your computer works, how to navigate around the computer storage structure, download software and files, and install programs, this should be a straightforward process.

If you already have Python 3 installed on your computer, you can skip this section and proceed at the next section, The Python shell.

Download the right software

You can download the official Python programming tools from python.org. On your computer browser, go to http://www.python.org/download/and get the latest version of Python (it should be version 3).

Before you can begin the installation, take some time to read the resources on https://wiki.python.org/moin/BeginnersGuide and make sure that you know the operating system (and version) of your computer and whether it is a 32-bit or a 64-bit. This is important to ensure that you download the right software.

The python.org/ downloads/ download page.

At the time of writing this book, the newest version of Python is Python 3.6.1. If you are unsure which version to download, click on the name of your operating system to access more options.

Windows installation

Installation is pretty straightforward on a Windows 10 or 7 computer. Simply download the right version of Python and open the installation wizard when the download is complete.

When the installation is complete, make sure that you check the **"Add Python 3.6 to PATH"** option in the last step of setup.

If the installation went well, you can launch Python from the Windows Start menu. The Python Integrated Development Environment (IDLE) shortcut is placed here:

Start ➤ Programs ➤ Python2 ➤ IDLE (Python GUI).

Linux and UNIX

For Linux and most Unix-based systems such as Mac OSX, the Python interpreter comes pre-loaded with the operating system. However, yours is most likely an older version of Python (version 2) which we will not be using in this guide. To find out the version of the Python Interpreter on your system, enter the following command on the terminal:

```
$ python
```

This command should initiate the interactive Python interpreter, which will display the version and other details.

To find out if Python 3 is installed, enter the command:

```
$ python3
```

You will probably get an error *"bash: python: command not found"* if version 3 of the Python interpreter is not installed in your computer. This means you will have to download and install it yourself but remember to check the **"Add**

Python 3.6 to PATH" option in the last step of setup when the installation is complete. Use the package manager if you are on a Debian-based Linux.

If you have a Mac, open the terminal application and enter the "python" command to start it. If the older version 2.x is installed, do not tamper with it because it used by the operating system in different ways. Instead, you can download the newest version from python.org/downloads/ or use Fink (http://finkproject.org) or MacPorts (http://macports.org) distribution tools.

Installation directory and exercise files

Note the installation folder of your Python interpreter because we are going to refer to that directory a lot in this course. This eBook comes with a set of python script files (.py files) bundled with the book; you should extract the folder in Python's installation folder to make it easily accessible from the command line. If you are a windows user, the path to the exercises directory should resemble this:

C:\Python36-21\ExFiles

You should also make it a habit to save your .py script files in this or similar location for easier access and execution.

The Python shell

Python offers a graphical user interface programming environment (Python IDLE) whose shortcut is placed on the desktop, start menu, or the app dock. This environment includes a text editor where you can write your code.

When you properly set up the Python Interpreter, you should be able to run any python files with the extension .py in any location from the command line. This is the approach we will use in this eBook. We believe it is best to learn using the terminal (command line) and a text editor of your choosing because it helps you master concepts and even exercise them with minimal distractions.

As an example, to if you have extracted the zipped exercises that accompany this eBook in the directory /*ExFiles*/ within the Python installation folder, you should be able to run the first exercise script with the name *Ex1*.py by typing:

```
$ python /ExFiles/Ex1.py
```

If you are a Mac or Linux user, depending on the installed versions of the Python interpreter, you may have to use the command:

```
$ python3 /ExFiles/Ex1.py
```

Install a text editor

Python code is entered in a plain text editor and saved in a file with the extension *.py*. There are quite a number of text editors popular with programmers that you can download and use for free. Word processor such as MS Word or WPS Writer do not work in creating scripts because they introduce special characters in the code that interfere with its execution. Some of the top text editors you should consider are:

- Notepad++
- Text Wrangler (Mac)
- Sublime Text
- Vim
- Atom

Remember that when Python 3 is set up in your computer, you have to figure out which command to use on the command line to call the interpreter (python for windows, or python3 for Linux and UNIX-based systems with Python 2.x installed). This book assumes that you use the command **python** on the command line to initialize the interpreter. If this is not the case for your computer, simply substitute it with **python3** to initialize the python interpreter.

Once you master this and have a text editor installed, you are set and ready to become a budding programmer.

Chapter 2: Hello World and the Basics of Python

Python shares many similarities with other object-oriented programming languages especially Perl, C, C++, and Java.

Interactive Programming Mode

On top of the list of similarities that Python shares with other top programming languages is the **Interactive Programming Mode**. This simply means that you can invoke the Python interpreter without passing a script file as a parameter.

Python Interactive Mode Programming

In this mode, you can execute commands straight on the interpreter. For instance, when you are on the Python interpreter enter the following code and press enter:

```
print ("Hello World!")
2 + 3
print ("My name is John!")
```

What result does entering the three codes above give you? You should see something like this:

```
print ("Hello World!")
'Hello World!'
2 + 3
5
print ("My name is John!")
'My name is John!'
```

As you can see, you can execute commands on the Python interpreter without saving your syntax in a script file. The Python interpreter can carry out arithmetic operations and other commands you enter directly into the terminal. Note, however, that in this mode, nothing will be saved permanently.

Script Programming Mode

For the rest of this ebook, we will use the script programming mode to execute program instructions and commands. What this means is that we will write the code in a script file (in this case a .py file) then save it and run it from the interpreter.

Creating the HelloWorld.py script file

Start your text editor and enter the following code exactly as it appears:

Ex1: Hello World

```
print ("Hello World!")
print ('I am now a Python programmer!')
```

This is a simple Python script with two lines. You can save this script as "*HelloWorld.py*" in your preferred location (preferably in a directory within the directory Python is installed or somewhere easily accessible like the desktop).

Remember the file's exact name because Python is case sensitive and *HelloWorld.py* is not the same as *helloworld.py*. Run the saved script from the command line (terminal) as explained below.

When saving a Python script, do not forget to include the .py extension at the end of the file name.

Note: This exercise also assumes that you already set the PATH variable in your computer (see installation instructions).

The demo script for this exercise is saved as *Ex1.py* in the archive of Python scripts that came with this book.

Running the HelloWorld.py script file

Now run the *HelloWorld.py* script from the command line (terminal) by following these steps:

When the python script file is saved, you can run it by invoking the Python interpreter in the location that the file is stored. For instance, if you saved it in the folder '*ExFiles*' within the installation directory of Python or the desktop, and you invoke the Python 3 interpreter using the keyword **python**, your command to run the HelloWorld.py script on the terminal (command line) would look like this:

```
$ python HelloWorld.py
```

What happens when you run the saved script? Does the terminal display the texts you entered after the keyword print and between brackets and quotation marks? Does it matter that you used single (') or a double ("") quotation marks?

Python Identifiers

When writing a program in Python, you will get used to entering common English words you are used to in everyday language, but with sometimes subtle noticeable differences and rules. When specifying a variable, a class, a module, a function or some other object (all of which we will learn later), you need to assign it an identifying name or simply an identifier.

Identifiers in Python must begin with an alphabetic letter (A-Z, a-z) or an underscore (_), followed by other letters and digits (0-9) or underscores. You cannot use punctuation characters and other symbols e.g. @, #, $, % and others within the identifier.

Also, because Python is case sensitive, uppercase and lowercase letters are different. For instance, *Hello* is not the same as *hello*.

Here are very vital conventions used to name identifiers in Python that you should know:

- A Class name must start with an uppercase letter. Every other identifier may start with a lowercase letter.
- An identifier that starts with a single leading underscore indicates that the identifier is private e.g. **_private**.
- An identifier that starts with two underscores is a strong private identifier.
- If an identifier ends with two trailing underscores, then it is a language-defined special name.

Reserved Words

Python has a set of English and non-English words reserved for the interpreter that you cannot use as variable, constant, or any other identifier names. Here is a table of these words:

and	as	assert	break	class
continue	def	del	elif	else
except	exec	finally	for	from
global	if	Import	in	is
lambda	not	or	pass	print
raise	while	return	try	with
Yield				

Table 1: Reserved keywords in Python

Lines and indentation

In other programming languages, curly braces ({}) or square brackets ([]) are used to group blocks of related code for function or class definition. In Python, blocks of code are denoted by a line indentation. This indentation rule is rigidly enforced and you can use a tab or a number of spaces, just as long as there is uniformity and consistency in their use. Consider these two blocks of code:

```
if True:
    print ("True")
    print ("Proceed")
else:
    print ("False")
```

The statements print ("True") and print ("Proceed") are indented with the same number of spaces. This means they form a block.

Note. These are very important syntax rules, but do not struggle to understand them all at this point. Just make sure you know what a block of code is and why blocks are important.

Comments in Python

Comments in a Python script are notes left by the programmer for later or for other programmers to understand the code. Comments in Python have the # sign at the beginning. Anything beyond the # sign to the end of the line will be ignored by the interpreter.

```python
print ("Hello World!") # Displays "Hello World!" on the screen.

# This line will also be ignored by the interpreter.

print ('I am now a Python programmer.') # This is another comment.
```

A comment can be typed on a new line or on the same line after an expression or a statement. You cannot write a comment that spans multiple lines on Python.

Quotation in Python

You can use a single ('), a double ("), or triple (''' or """) quotation marks to denote string literals in Python. The only rule is that you must start and end with the same type of quotation on a string.

Triple quotations are used when the string of text spans over multiple lines.

```python
print ('Hello World!') # Double quotation marks.
```

```
print ("I am now a Python programmer.") # his line will also be ignored
by the interpreter.

print ("""I am now a Python programmer.

        This means I should be able to create a simple Python

        Script and run it with no difficulty.""")
```

Blank Lines

A blank line is a line that contains only whitespace, commonly inserted into code for aesthetic purposes and to keep the code organized. The Python interpreter completely ignores a blank line in the script.

There must be a blank line after a multi-line string block to terminate the statement.

Chapter 3: Variables and Basic Operators in Python

Types of Variables in Python

In object-oriented programming, a variable is a space in computer memory that is reserved for storing values of a specified type. When you declare a variable in your Python script, you are essentially asking the interpreter to allocate computer memory for the type of data expected and you assign that memory location a name. This name is what we call a **variable name** and it may be assigned any of the following five data types supported by Python:

1. Numbers
2. Strings
3. Lists
4. Tuples
5. Dictionary

We will cover each of these variables in detail in Chapters 3, 4, and 5.

The interpreter decides which data will be stored in the reserved memory based on the data type declaration. It is therefore important to specify the type of data the variable will store so that the interpreter can allocate sufficient memory space.

Declaring a variable

You declare a variable in Python by assigning a variable name a value. Unlike various other high level programming languages, with Python, you do not need to explicitly declare a memory space reservation, it happens automatically when a value is assigned to the variable using the equal sign (=) called the assignment operator in programming.

Ex2

Enter the following code in your editor and run it from the command line:

```
name = "Peter"

age = 22

score = 97.21


print (name, "is", age, "years old.")

print (name, "scored", score, "percent.")
```

The print statement is to display the values of the variable as proof of the assignment. What does your program display when you run the script?

In the statement name = *"Peter"*, the operand **'name'** on the left side of the equal sign is the variable name while that on the right, in this case **"Peter"**, is the value of the variable.

You can see that the value of variable **name** is enclosed in quotation marks while the values of variables **age** and **score** are not. Do not worry about this, we will look at why in detail when discussing string and number data types in the next chapter of the book.

Assigning a single value to multiple variables

One of the things that make Python such an efficient and simple languages is that you can assign several variables a single value in one statement.

Ex3

```
x = y = z = 10
print (x)
print (y)
```

```
print (z)
```

When you run the code in Ex3, you will realize when the values of variables x, y, and z are displayed on the screen, are all the same (10). The integer objects x, y, and z are created in the same memory location when the value 10 is assigned to them. This is how you associate one value with multiple variables.

Assigning multiple variables multiple values

Just the way you can assign multiple variables one value using one statement in Python, you can also assign multiple objects to multiple variables with ease. Your code would look like Ex4:

Ex4

```
name, age, score = "Peter", 22, 97.21
print (age, "year old", name, "scored", score, "percent.")
```

In this exercise, you assign the same values we used in Ex2 to the same variables, except in a single line of code.

Basic Operators

An operator is a construct that is used to manipulate the value of an operand. Most of the operators you will encounter while learning Python will look familiar to you from math class, and most serve the same purpose as it did when you were introduced to them in school.

In the expression 5 + 6, 5 and 6 are the operands and the + (plus) is the operator.

The Python language supports seven types of operators:

- Arithmetic operators

- Assignment operators

- Relational or comparison operators

- Logical Operators

- Membership operators

- Identity operators

- Bitwise operators

In this book, we will cover a brief introduction of the first six operators with brief example scripts that put them in practice.

1. Arithmetic operators

As the name hints, arithmetic operators are the same ones you learned in Math, albeit with a few changes. They are:

Operator	Name	Function
+	Addition	Adds the values of both operands.
-	Subtraction	Subtracts the value of the right operand from the value of the left operand.
*	Multiplication	Multiplies the values of both operands.
/	Division	Divides the value of the left operand by the value of the right operand.
%	Modulus	Like division above, except that it returns the remainder value after division.

	Floor Division	Like division above, except that it returns the quotient value without the decimal point digits.
//		
**	Exponent	Calculates the exponential calculation (power) on the operands

Table 2: Arithmetic operators in Python

Ex5

```
x = 12
y = 8

print ("When x = 12 and y = 8:")

z = x + y
print ("1: x + y is", z)

z = x - y
print ("2: x - y is", z)

z = x * y
print ("3: x * b is", z)

z = x / y
print ("4: x / b is ", z)
```

```
z = x % y
print ("5: x % y is ", z)


a, b = 3, 2
print ("Given a, b = 3, 2:")


c = a**b
print ("1: a**b is ", c)


c = a//b
print ("2: a//b is ", c)
```

2. Assignment operators

Assignment operators in Python do just what the name suggests: assign values. An assignment operator will assign the value of the right operand to the left operand.

Symbol	Name	Function
=	Equal	Assigns the value of the right operand to the left operand.
+=	Add AND	Adds the value of both operand and assigns the result to the left operand.
-=	Subtract AND	Subtracts the value of the right operand from that of the left and assigns the result to the left operand

	Multiply AND	Multiplies the value of both operands and assigns the result to the left operand.
*=		
/=	Divide AND	Divides the value of the left operand with that of the right and assigns the result to the left operand.
%=	Modulus AND	It takes modulus using the two operands and assigns the result to the left operand.
**=	Exponent AND	Finds the power (exponential) of the left operand by the right and assigns the result to the left operand.
//=	Floor Division	Performs a floor division on the operands and assigns the
	AND	result to the left operand.

Table 3: Assignment operators in Python

Ex6

```
x = 10
y = 5

print ("If x = 10 and y = 5:")

z = x + y
print ("1: x + y is", z)

z += x
print ("2: += x is", z)
```

```
z *= x
print ("3: *= x is", z)


z /= x
print ("4: /= x is", z)


a = 2


print ("Given a, x = 2, 10:")


a %= x
print ("5: a %= x is", a)


a **= x
print ("6: **= x is", z)


a //= x
print ("7: //= x is", a)
```

3. Relational (comparison) operators

A comparison operator simply compares the value of the left operand with that of the right operand and determines how they relate.

Operator	Name	Function
==	Equal to	Condition becomes True if the value of the left operand is equal to the value of the right operand.

!=	Not equal to	Condition becomes True if the value of the left operand is not equal to the value of the right operand.
>	Greater than	Condition becomes True if the value of the left operand is greater than the value of the right operand.
<	Less than	Condition becomes True if the value of the left operand is less than the value of the right operand.
>=	Equal to or greater than	Condition becomes True if the value of the left operand is equal to or greater than the value of the right operand.
<=	Equal to or less than	Condition becomes True if the value of the left operand is equal to or less than the value of the right operand.

Table 4: Relational (comparison) operators in Python.

Ex7

```
number1 = 100 > 50;

number2 = 100 < 50;

number3 = 100 == 50;

number4 = 100 != 50;

number5 = 100 >= 50;

number6 = 100 <= 50;
```

```
print ("1. Value of number1:", number1)

print ("2. Value of number2:", number2)

print ("3. Value of number3:", number3)

print ("4. Value of number4:", number4)

print ("5. Value of number5:", number5)

print ("6. Value of number6:", number6)
```

4. Logical operators

Also called boolean operators, logical operators are statements that evaluate to either of the two boolean conditions: **True** or **False**. The **not** keyword introduced as a reserved keyword earlier reverses a boolean type, **True** to **False** and vice versa.

Operator	Function
and	Returns **True** if both operands are True.
or	Returns **True** if either of the operands are true.
not	Returns **True** if operand False and False if it is True.

Table 5: Logical operators in Python

Ex8

```
x = True

y = False
```

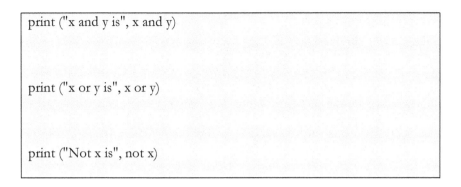

```
print ("x and y is", x and y)


print ("x or y is", x or y)


print ("Not x is", not x)
```

5. Membership operators

The two membership operators in Python check for the operand's presence in a sequence of values such as strings (alphanumeric characters), lists, or tuples.

Operator	Function
in	Returns True if the operand is found in the specified sequence and False if it is not found.
not in	Returns True if the operand is not found in the specified sequence and False if it is found.

Table 6: Membership operators in Python

Ex 9

```
x = "Python Programming"
y = {1:"h", 2:"m"}



print ("y" in x)
```

```
print ("o" not in x)



print (1 in y)



print ("a" in y)
```

6. Identity Operators

An identity operator compares the memory locations of two objects. There are two identical operators:

Operator	Function
is	Returns **True** if both operands point to the same object and **False** if they do not.
is not	Returns **False** if both operands point to the same object and **False** if they do not.

Table 7: Identity operators in Python

Ex10

```
a = 10

a1 = 10

b = "Holla"

b1 = "holla"

c = [1,2,3]

c1 = [1,2,3]
```

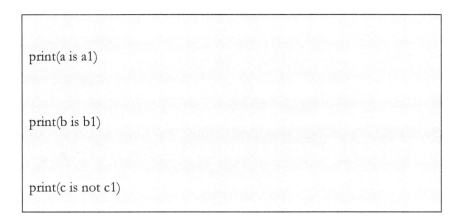

7. Bitwise operators

Bitwise operators are used bit-by-bit operators that execute operations on operands in binary form.

Symbol	Operator	Function
&	AND	Copies a bit if found in both operands.
|	OR	Copies a bit if found in either of the operands.
~	NOT	Complements an operand by flipping ones for zeros and zeros for ones
^	XOR	Copies a bit if set in only one operand.
>>	Shift right	The value of the left operand is moved right by the value of bits in the left operand.
<<	Shift left	The value of the left operand is moved left by the number of bits in the right operand.

Table 8: Bitwise operators in Python

Operators Precedence in Python

The Python interpreter follows a very strict order of execution when presented with multiple operations. The table below summarizes all the operations in order of precedence from the highest to the lowest.

Order	Operation	Function
1	()	Operations enclosed in brackets are executed first.
2	**	Exponentiation (raise to the power)
3	~ + -	Complement, unary plus (+@) and minus (-@)
4	* / % //	Multiply, divide, modulus and floor division
5	+ -	Addition and subtraction
6	>> <<	Bitwise shift right and left
7	&	Bitwise AND
8	| ^	OR and Bitwise exclusive OR
9	<= < > >=	Comparison operators
10	<> == !=	Relational operators
11	= %= /= //= -= += *= **=	Assignment operators

12	is is not	Identity operators
13	in not in	Membership operators
14	not or and	Logical operators

Table 9: Operators precedence in Python

Chapter 4: Working with Strings and Numbers

In Chapter 2, we touched lightly on the five basic data types that you will be learning to work with in the course of this book. By the end of this chapter, you will be able to work with the two most popular data types: numbers and strings.

Strings in Python

The first data type we encountered in the first exercise of this book. It is a sequence of characters including symbols and alphanumeric characters. In chapter 2, you learned that you can use a single ('), a double ("), or triple ('" or """) quotation marks to denote a string.

If you have been practicing what you have learned so far, I am sure you have created countless string variables in your scripts. However, so far we have only touched on how to display them using the method *print*. In this section, we will look at a number of other great things you can do with strings.

Creating a string

You create a string by enclosing characters in quotation marks and assigning it a variable name. In the first exercise, we created a string object and displayed its contents on the screen. In **Ex2**, we created one string object called **name** with value **"Peter"**.

You can also create a string object by formatting a user's input using the method *str()* (we will cover this later). In Ex11 below, for instance, the user will be prompted to enter a string of text which is assigned the variable **name**.

Accessing the values of a string

In Python, you can access the individual characters of a string using slicing, indexing, and a range of other operations. If you try to access a character that is out of index range, you will get an **IndexError**. The indexes of the characters start at 0 for the first character and you can only use positive integers. If you try to use any other number type such as a decimal (float) you will encounter a *TypeError*

Ex11

```
name = input("Enter a word longer than 5 letters: ")


print (name[0], "is the first indexed character.")

print (name[1], "is the second indexed character.")

print (name[2:4], "is the range of third to fifth character.")

print (name[-1], "is the last character.")

print (name[-2], "is the second to last character.")
```

As you can see in the example above, you can slice the characters in a string using a square bracket ([]) and even specify a range of characters using colons ([:]).

Ex12

```
name = "Peter"

print (name)

name = "Peter Pan"

print (name)
```

In *Ex12*, first we assign the variable *name* the string *Peter* and to see it we use the print method. We then re-assign the string Peter Pan the same variable and it is updated.

String concatenation and iteration

You can join two or more strings to make them one using the plus operator (+) or separating named string variables with a comma. For instance, here is another way we could have updated the name variable in Ex12.py:

```
name = "Peter"

print (name)

name = name[0:4]+" Pan"

print (name)
```

You can repeat multiple copies of one string to create new strings using the asterisk operator * as in Ex13.

Ex13

```
string1 = "Hello"

string2 = "World"

string3 = "!"


print ("string1 * 3 + string3 = ", string1 * 3 + string3)

print ("string1 + string2 = ", string1 + string2)

print ("string1, string2 = ", string1, string2)

print ("string1, string2 + string3 = ", string1, string2 + string3)
```

Do you notice how the use of a plus or comma determines whether a space is put between the two strings or not?

String escape sequence

You can now work with almost any type of text, after all, you just need to enclose them in quotation marks and split, slice, iterate etc. But what do you do when you want to work with a string that has quotation marks. For instance, how would you print a text that reads:

"I am sorry," he said, "the 'Transformers' toys are out of stock".

Notice that this sentence has both double and single quotation marks that create a string. If you slap quotation marks on this string and try to print it, you will encounter a Syntax error. Try it.

In such a case, we can either use triple quotation marks or escape sequences to get around this problem. An escape sequence begins with a backslash (\). You will place the backslash in front of all double quotes inside a string if the string is created with double quotation marks. You will do the same for single quotation marks if the string is created with single quotation marks.

Ex14

```
print ("I am sorry,\" he said, \"the 'Transformers' toys are out of
stock\".")
print ('"I am sorry," he said, "the \'Transformers\' toys are out of stock".')
print ("""

        "I am sorry," he said, "the 'Transformers' toys are out of stock".

    """)
```

There are quite a few of other escape sequences that you will encounter as you practice working with strings. Here is a tabulated list of the most popular escape sequences you will encounter and what they do.

Character	Sequence	Description
\\	Backslash	Prints one backlash.
\"	Double quote	Prints a double quote.
\'	Single quote	Prints a single quote.
\a	Bell	Sounds the system bell.
\b	Backspace	Moves the cursor back one space
\t	Tab	Moves the cursor forward one tab.
\n	Newline	Moves the cursor to the beginning of the next line

Table 10: String literal escape characters in Python.

String Methods

There are quite a number of methods you can use to manipulate strings in Python. Some of the most popular are included in the table below:

Method	Description
upper()	Returns the uppercase characters of a string.
lower()	Returns the lowercase version of a string.
swapcase()	Like toggle case in word processing, it returns a new string with the case of each character in a string switched.
capitalize()	Capitalizes the first letter of string.
title()	Returns a string with the first character of each word capitalized and the rest lowercase.

strip()	Returns a string with all white spaces including spaces, newlines, and tabs at the beginning and the end removed.
split()	Splits all words into a list.
join()	Joins all words into a string.

Table 11: String methods in Python

Ex15

```
mytext = "Happy new year World!"


print ("mytext.upper() = ", mytext.upper())

print ("mytext.lower() = ", mytext.lower())

print ("mytext.swapcase() = ", mytext.swapcase())

print ("mytext.capitalize() = ", mytext.capitalize())

print ("mytext.title() = ", mytext.title())

print ("mytext.strip() = ", mytext.strip())

print ("mytext.split() = ", mytext.split())
```

String formatting

In Python, you can format a string by placing the string formatting operator (%) to the left of the conversion specifier, and the values to the right. You can use this formatting operator on a string containing different data types including tuples, lists, and dictionaries.

Ex16

```
name = "Peter"

score = 75

print ("My name is %s and I scored %d percent!" %(name, score))
```

In this example, we use the placeholders *%s* and *%d* to format the strings using placeholders *%s* for string and *%d* for decimal integer. The table below presents the format symbols you will use on different data types.

Format Symbol	Conversion
%c	character
%s	string (converted using str() before formatting)
%i or %d	signed decimal integer
%u	unsigned decimal integer
%o	octal integer
%x	hexadecimal integer (lowercase characters)
%X	hexadecimal integer (UPPERcase characters)
%e	exponential notation (lowercase 'e')
%E	exponential notation (UPPERcase 'E')
%f	floating point real number
%g	the shorter of %f and %e
%G	the shorter of %f and %E

Table 12: String formatting symbols

Checking membership in a string

The membership operators **in** and **not in** you were introduced to in the previous chapter can be used on sequential data types including strings. You will learn how to use these operators on strings when we cover how to apply them on lists and tuples in the next chapter.

Numbers in Python

After strings, numbers are the next most popular value types in Python. Python supports three types of numbers: integers, floating point numbers, and complex numbers defined as *int*, *float*, and *complex* respectively. Just like strings, number data types are immutable.

An integer is a whole number without a decimal point while a floating point number has a decimal. For instance, 2 is an integer while 2.0 is a floating point number. In Python, integers can be of any length and floats are accurate up to 15 places.

Complex numbers are in the form $x + yj$ where x is the real part of the number and y is the imaginary part. Complex numbers is beyond the scope of this book so we will cover only integers and floats.

We deal with decimal (base 10) numbers in our everyday lives. However, as you become a proficient programmer, you will need to know how to program systems using only binary (base 2), octal (base 8), and hexadecimal (base16) numbers. Again, this book only works with what we are all used to: base 10 numbers.

Using mathematical operators on numbers

With Python, you can carry out almost any calculation with numbers without adding any extra code. For instance, on IDLE or the Terminal, you can enter mathematical operations directly and the interpreter will return the results.

Ex17

```
my_math = 10 * -5

print (my_math)

print ("10 + 12 * 3 = ", 10 + 12 * 3)

print ("15 + 8 = ", 15 + 8)

print ("15 + 8.0 = ", 15 + 8.0)

print ("217 %5 = ", 217 %5)
```

A number variable is created by assigning a number a name using the equal sign (=). In the above example, we created a variable called **my_math** with the value **10*-5**.

You can see in Ex17 that when you use two integer operands, the result will be an integer and when you use an integer and a float or two float operands, the result will be a float. You can get more practice on this by trying the different types of operators we covered in Chapter 3.

Number coercion

The process of converting from one type of number to another is called coercion. You already discovered that operations such as addition, subtraction, division, multiplication, and others implicitly coerce an integer to a float if one of the operands is a float.

You can also use the built-in functions **int()**, **float()**, and **complex()** to explicitly coerce between number types and from strings.

Ex18

```
number1 = 12

number2 = 2.5
```

```
string1 = "10"


print (float(number1)) #convert number1 to float and print

print (int(number2)) #Convert number2 to integer and print

print (int(string1) * number2)


YoB = int(input("Enter your year of birth as YYYY: "))

age = 2017 - YoB


print ("You are %d years old!" %age)
```

In Ex18, the variable number1 is an integer, number2 is a float, and string1 is a string. The 5th line of the script converts number1 to the type float, the next converts number2 to an integer, and the 7th line converts string1 into an integer before multiplying by number2. Note that when converting a number from a float to an integer, it gets truncated at the decimal point, not truncated.

In the same example, notice that we created the variable **YoB** by asking the user to *"Enter your year of birth as YYYY: "* then converting it to an integer before working with it.

Mathematical Functions

There are many inbuilt Python functions that perform mathematical operations on numbers. To use mathematical functions in the standard module, you will have to import the math module using ***import math***.

Some of the most common you should know about are tabulated in Table 13 below:

Function	Description
fabs(x)	Returns the absolute value of x (positive distance between 0 and x)
ceil(x)	Returns the ceiling value of x (the smallest integer that is not less than x)
floor(x)	Returns the floor value of x (largest integer that is not greater than x)
cmp(x, y)	Compares x and y and returns 1 (if x > y), 0 if x == y, or -1 if x < y
exp(x)	Returns the exponential of x (ex)
Pow(x,y)	Returns the value of x**y
min(x,y)	Returns the smallest of the numbers x and y
max(x,y)	Returns the largest of the numbers x and y
sqrt(x)	Returns the square root of x when x > 0.
pi	Mathematical constant pi
e	Mathematical constant e

Table 13: Mathematical Functions

Chapter 5: Lists and Tuples and Dictionary

Lists and tuples are popular compound data types that generally fall into the sequences category alongside strings, byte sequences, byte arrays, and range objects (you will learn about these at intermediate and advanced stages). Strings may look a lot different from lists and tuples as you will notice, but they are similar in that:

- Their elements are placed in a defined sequence.
- The elements can be accessed via indices.
- They can be manipulated via slicing using []

Python, unlike other object-oriented programming languages, uses the same syntax and function names to manipulate list and tuple sequential data types. These operations include indexing, slicing, iteration, concatenation, and checking for membership. We will cover each of these in greater detail in this section.

Python Lists and Tuples

A list in Python is a mutable type that is made up of a collection of ordered objects. The objects contained in a list do not have to be of the same type and may include other lists (nested sublists).

A tuple, on the other hand, unlike a list, is an immutable type. This means that the objects (items) in a tuple cannot be changed once created. Just like a list, the objects in a tuple can be of different types.

Creating a list and tuple

A list is created by placing all the objects (or items) inside a square bracket [] and separated by commas. A tuple is created by separating its values with a comma only but it is a good practice to enclose them in parentheses (brackets).

Ex 19

```
list1 = ["March", "Five", 2012, 19.25, "Heaven"]

tuple1 = ("a", "Sydney", "1900", 3.142, 0.01, "Python")

tuple2 = "x", "empire", "lego", 1, 2.0, 7



print (list1)

print (tuple1)

print (tuple2)
```

You can also create a list by splitting the elements of a string as we saw in Ex15.

Accessing values in lists and tuples

You access the values of lists and tuples (separated by commas) the same way we did the characters of a string: using indices and slicing with square brackets. Consider the operations in Ex20:

Ex20

```
list1 = ["March", "Five", 2012, 19.25, "Heaven"]

tuple1 = ("a", "Sydney", "1900", 3.142, 0.01, "Python")

tuple2 = "x", "empire", "lego", 1, 2.0, 7



print (list1[0:2])

print (list1[2:])
```

```
print (tuple1[1:5])

print (tuple2[0:-1])
```

You can see that we use the same slicing operations and indexes on *list1*, *tuple1*, and *tuple2* as we did strings. You will also remember that indexes start at 0 but you can use negative indexes to count from the last object (-1).

Updating list objects

Because lists in Python are a mutable type, you can update a single or multiple elements using the assignment operator (=). You can also add new items on the list using the *append()* method as in *Ex21*.

Ex21

```
list1 = ["March", "Five", 2012, 19.25, "Heaven"]


print ("Old list1: ", list1)


list1[0] = "December"

list1[-1] = "Hell"

list1.append("Computer")


print ("New list1: ", list1)
```

You can see in the example above that we updated *list1* with new items at positions *[0]* (first) and *[-1]* (last) then added a new item after the last using *list.append()*.

Tuples are immutable and cannot be updated. However, you can take the values of a tuple and create a new tuple by adding new items or combining with an existing tuple.

Deleting list objects

There are two ways to delete items from a list in Python. If you know the exact items to delete, you can use the del statement but if you don't know you can use the *remove()* method. Consider their application in Ex22 below:

Ex22

```
list1 = ["March", "Five", 2012, 19.25, "Heaven"]


print ("Old list1: ", list1)


del list1[3]

list1.remove("Five")


print ("New list1: ", list1)
```

Basic list and tuple operations

Much like strings, lists and tuples respond to the concatenation (+) and iteration (*) operations.

Ex23

```
list1 = ["March", "Five", 2012, 19.25, "Heaven"]

list2 = ["Mayday", "rocket", -60]

tuple1 = ("a", "Sydney", "1900", 3.142, 0.01, "Python")


print (len(list1))

print (len(tuple1))


list3 = list1 + list2


print (list3)

print (list*2)
```

Python comes with a range of in-built functions that you can use to manipulate lists and tuples, a good example being the ***len()***, ***(len(list1)***, and ***len(tuple1))*** functions in Ex23 above. Others are:

Function	Description
cmp()	Compares the objects of two lists or tuples.
len()	Returns the total length of a sequence.
max()	Returns the item with the highest value in a sequence
min()	Returns the item with the lowest value in a sequence

| list(seq) | Converts from a tuple type to a list. |
| tuple(seq) | Converts from a list type to a tuple. |

Table 14: List and tuple functions.

Python list methods

As far as list methods go, we have only used two so far: ***append()*** in ***Ex21*** and ***remove()*** in ***Ex22***. There are more you should play around with when practicing what you have learned about lists. Here is a table of list methods in Python and what they do.

Method	Definition
append()	Adds an item to the end of the list
remove()	Removes an item from the list
extend()	Adds all elements of a list to another list
insert()	Inserts an item at the defined index
copy()	Returns a shallow copy of a list
pop()	Removes an item at the given index and returns it
index()	Returns the index of the first matched item
clear()	Removes all items on a list
count()	Returns the number of items passed as an argument
reverse()	Reverses the order of items in a list
sort()	Sorts items in a list in ascending order

Table 15: List methods in Python

Can you apply these methods to strings and tuples to find out which ones work (and why)?

Advantages of tuples over lists

We have established that lists and tuples are similar in many ways, and they can be used interchangeably in many situations. Considering that lists are mutable while tuples are not, most beginners often wonder under what situations a tuple is more applicable compared to a list. There are four:

1. When working with heterogeneous (different) types of data, it is better to use a tuple. A list is more practical when sequencing data of the same type.
2. Where the sequence will be iterated, it is more advantageous to use a tuple because it is immutable and will be iterated faster by the interpreter.
3. A tuple can be used as a dictionary key because its data is immutable. A list cannot be used as a dictionary key.
4. When you have data that does not change, the best way to make sure that it does not change is to implement it as a tuple.

Python Dictionaries

It would be impractical to write a functional computer program in Python without using the sequential data types we have covered so far (strings, lists, and tuples) and dictionaries.

Like lists, dictionaries are a mutable data type whose objects can easily be deleted, updated, and added at runtime and they can also contain different types of data (including lists). The difference between the two is that dictionaries contain items not in any order, unlike lists whose items are ordered. This means that the items on a dictionary are accessed using keys and not their positions.

We can therefore say that a dictionary in python is an associative array or hash in which each value is mapped to (associated with) a key.

Creating a dictionary

A dictionary in Python is created by pairing values with keys using a colon in the format (key:value). The key:value pairs of items are separated by commas and are enclosed in curly braces ({}). A dictionary can also be created or converted from another data type using the built in function *dict()*. In *Ex23*, we have created three dictionaries called myDict, dict1, and class_performance

Ex23

```
myDict = {"ID":12, "name":"John Daniel", "score":95, "Grade":"A"}


dict1 = dict([(1, "cars"), (2, "computers"), (3, "planes")])


class_performance = dict({1:"Mark", 2:"Janet", 3:"Simon", 4:"Arthur",
5:"Lee"})


print (myDict)

print (dict1)

print (class_performance)
```

Accessing dictionary elements

As mentioned earlier, while indexing is used to access the values of sequential data types, keys are used to access the values of a dictionary. You can use just the key inside a square bracket but it is recommended that you make it a habit to use the *get()* method.

Ex24

```
myDict = {"ID":12, "name":"John Daniel", "score":95, "Grade":"A"}


print (myDict["name"])


print (myDict.get("score"))
```

Using *get()* has the advantage of returning a None value when a key is missing and not a KeyError you would encounter using the keys in square brackets.

Updating the dictionary

Because the dictionary is a mutable type, you can add new items, delete existing ones, or update keys and values using the assignment operator (=).

Ex25

```
myDict = {"ID":12, "name":"John Daniel", "score":95, "Grade":"A"}


print ("Old myDict: ", myDict)
```

```
myDict["YOB"] = 1995

myDict["Grade"] = "B"

del myDict["ID"]


print ("New myDict: ", myDict)
```

In the example, we added a new dictionary key:value pair **"YOB":1995** and updated **"Grade"** key value to **B**. We also used **del** to delete the **"ID"**:12 pair. To clear all the dictionary entries, you can use **dict.clear** function or **del dict** to delete the entire dictionary.

Dictionary methods

Here is a table of the methods available with the dictionary type in Python alongside their definitions. Be sure to try out each of them to see that it does what is described.

Method	Description
dict.clear()	Removes all items form the dictionary.
dict.copy()	Returns a shallow copy of the dictionary.
dict.items()	Returns a new key:value view of the items in the dictionary.
dict.keys()	Returns a new view of the dictionary's keys.
dict.pop(key[,d])	Removes the item with key and return its value or d if key is not found.
dict.popitem()	Removes and returns an arbitary key:value item).

dict.update()	Updates the dictionary with the key:value pairs, overwriting existing keys.
dict.values()	Returns a new view of the dictionary's values

Table16: Dictionary methods in Python.

Dictionary functions

Python comes with a number of built-in dictionary functions that you can practice with to gain a deeper understanding what they do. They are:

Function	Description
all()	Returns True if all dictionary keys are **true** or if the dictionary is empty.
any()	Returns True if any key of the dictionary is **true** and **False** if the dictionary is empty.
len()	Returns the length of the dictionary (the number of items).
cmp()	Compares the items of two dictionaries.
sorted()	Returns a new sorted list of keys in the dictionary.
type(var)	Returns dictionary type if passed variable is of type dictionary.
str()	Produces a printable string of the dictionary items.

Table 17: Dictionary functions in Python.

Properties of dictionary keys in Python

Dictionary values can be arbitrary objects - standard or user-defined - there are no restrictions. However, there are two vital considerations to bear in mind about dictionary keys:

1. You cannot have two or more similar keys. Keys must be unique. When there are more than one similar keys, the last to be assigned is the only valid one.

2. Dictionary keys must be immutable. You can use numbers, strings, or tuples as keys but you cannot use something like ['key'].

Chapter 6: Input, Output, and Import

Python comes with numerous built-in functions readily available at the Python prompt to enable you write programs that accept user input and can output processed information. From the very first Hello World! program we wrote, we have used the print() output function and in Example11 we introduced the input() function to capture the user's keyboard input.

In this short chapter, we will go into detail on how to code the I/O processes in Python.

Capturing keyboard input using input()

The input() function reads data from the keyboard as a string, no matter whether it is enclosed in quotes ("" or '). You can convert the captured text into a specified data type using a casting function (see Example18 script) or using the eval function.

When the input() function is called, the interpreter will stop the program flow until the user provides an input and ends it by pressing the return key. The function offers an optional [prompt] parameter of text to print on the screen.

```
input([prompt])
```

The prompt text will be displayed to the left of the line where the user will need to enter keyboard characters. It is a good habit to end the prompt text with a colon and a space (:) to properly format the input area for the end user.

Ex26

```
name = input("Enter your name?: ")

age = int(input("Enter your age: "))
```

```
gender = input ("Are you Male or Female?: ")


print ("Hello,", name + ". You are a", age, "year old", gender + ".")
```

There is more you can do with input() besides capturing a single string of text. For instance, you can capture a sequence of data and save it as a list.

Ex27

```
my_cities = input("Name three cities you have lived in: ")


city1, city2, city3 = my_cities.split()


print ("Here are the cities you have lived in: \n1. ", city1, "\n2. ", city2,
"\n3. ", city3)
```

As you can see in this example, you can request user input using the input() function and perform further functions with the captured data such as split it to create a mutable sequential data type (list).

Printing to the screen using the print() function

Throughout this course, we have used the print() statement to display text on the computer screen. In principle, for any computer program to be useful, it must be able to communicate with the user by displaying requested information on the screen.

In Python 3, we use the print() function to convert expressions separated by commas into a string and display the result to the standard console output.

Arguments of the print function

The print function takes the following arguments:

```
print(value1, value2.., sep='', end='')
```

You can print an arbitrary number of values separated by commas as you can see in almost all the examples so far. The ***separator*** (sep) argument defines what separates the printed values and the ***end*** argument defines what characters or symbols are placed at the end of the string to print. Other arguments you will discover in the advanced stages of learning to write code in Python are file and flush.

Ex.28

```
name = input("What is your name? ")

my_cities = input("Name three cities you have lived in: ")


city1, city2, city3 = my_cities.split()


print ("\nIs your name really", name, end = "?\n\n")

print (name + ", you have lived in:", city2, city3, city1, sep = "\n", end = ".\n")
```

A print call is ended with a new line by default, but including the end argument overrides this.

Python Import

So far, the program examples we have been creating have been very small, only a few lines long. As you create longer scripts and bigger programs, you will find it necessary to break it into modules.

A module is a python file containing statements and definitions. Every Python module has a filename and ends with the .py extension, just like the scripts you have been creating so far. There are countless modules distributed with the standard Python installation package or created by individuals and downloadable from the internet.

To import a module in Python, you use the keyword ***import***.

Ex29

```
import math


r = float(input("Enter the radius of the circle: \n"))


area = (math.pi * r * r)

circumference = (2 * math.pi * r)


print ("Radius", r, sep = ": ", end = "cm.\n")

print ("Pi", math.pi, sep = ": ", end = ".\n")

print ("Area", area, sep = ": ", end = " sq. cm.\n")
```

```
print ("Circumference", circumference, sep = ": ", end = " cm.\n")
```

In Ex29, we imported the math module using the statement ***import math*** from which we found ***math.pi***. Here, we use the value of pi to calculate the area and circumference of a circle whose radius the user is prompted to enter and converted to a float number.

When we import a module, all the definitions it contains are available in the program's scope. As you practice using import, you will discover that you can also import specific attributes or functions using keywords. For instance, in our above example, we could have just imported the value of pi using the statement:

```
import math pi
```

You can also write the import statement like this:

```
from math import pi
```

Python searches all the directory locations defined in ***sys.path***. You can also import more than one module in one import statement. For instance, to view the list of directories defined in ***sys.path*** import the ***sys*** modules and use the print statement to display the path values.

Can you see the list of directories defined in the ***sys.path***?

Chapter 7: Decision Making and Looping

When writing a program, you will have to include decision making structures in anticipation of conditions that will occur during the execution of the program. In this chapter, you will learn how to use the if statement to write a program that makes decisions and how to create a program that iterate particular block of code until or when a condition is met.

Decision making in Python

Decision making structures evaluate one or multiple expressions that can return **True** or **False** outcomes then use the response to determine which action to take or block of code to execute when the outcome is **True** or **False**.

The general most basic decision making structure found in most programming languages take this format:

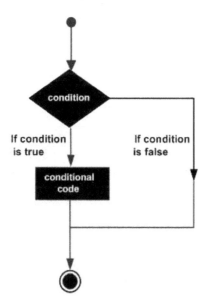

If the condition test returns any ***non-zero*** or ***non-null*** value, Python registers it as **True**. ***Null*** and ***Zero*** values are considered ***False***. The following types of decision making statements are available in Python:

1. if

2. if...else

3. if...elif...else

4. Nested if

The if statement

The if statement tests a condition such as if two variables are equal, then executes a block of code if the result is True. The most basic syntax of this statement is:

```
if <condition>:

    statement(s)
```

Take note of the trailing colon (:) after the test condition and the indentation of the next line of statement(s).

The statement(s) in this case is an indented block that may be made up of one or more statements. The indentation is very important in Python because this is how the interpreter determines which lines of code belong to what block. Make it a habit to indent your lines of code to one level using a Tab or four spaces.

The if statement tests the <condition> ***Boolean*** expression which will return either a ***True*** or ***False***. If the condition is ***True***, the statement(s) are executed and if it is ***False***, the interpreter will ignore the indented statements and continue with the program execution at the first line after the indented block of statement(s).

Ex30

```
number = int(input("Enter a number to check if it is EVEN: "))


if number % 2 == 0:

        print (number, "is an even number.")
```

Notice that in our example, when you enter a value that when tested returns False, the program quits because there are no statements to execute.

The condition can have more than one conditions to be evaluated using logical operators as in our next example.

Ex31

```
age = int(input("How old are you? "))

gender = str(input("Is your gender M or F? "))


if age >= 18 and gender == "M":

        print ("You are an adult male.")
```

The condition in this exercise checks if the value of age is equal to or greater than 18 and the value of gender is M to display the indented string statement.

The if...else statement

The if statement has one downside: that there is only one block of code to execute when the test condition evaluates to True. The if...else statement takes this structure:

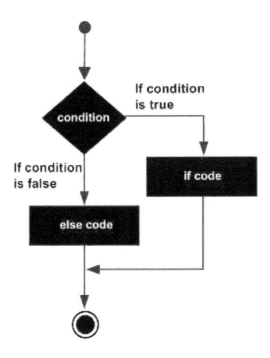

Here is the Python syntax for this decision making structure:

if <condition>:

statement(s)

else:

statement(s)

If the test condition returns **True**, the first block of statements is executed, and if the test condition returns False, the block of statements under the else: statement are executed.

For instance, the program in Example30 would be much more practical if it could tell us that number being evaluated is odd when it is not even rather than just terminating. To achieve this, we use the if...else statement instead of just if.

Ex32

```
number = int(input("Check this number if it is EVEN or ODD: "))


if number % 2 == 0:

        print (number, "is an even number.")

else:

        print (number, "is an odd number.")
```

The if...elif statement

The *if...elif* statement is a complex construct of the if...else conditional statement, *elif* being a shorthand for else if.

With the *if...elif* statement, there are more than one conditions to test and at the end of the tests is an optional *else:* statement. Beneath *else:*, just like with the previous *if...else* statement, is a block of code to execute if all the previous conditions return *False*.

The syntax for the if...elif decision making structure looks like this:

```
if <condition>:

statement(s)

elif:
```

```
statement(s)
```

Ex.33

```
age = int(input("How old are you? "))


if age < 0:

        print ("Age cannot be less than 0.")

elif age < 13:

        print ("You are a child.")

elif age < 20:

        print ("You are a teenager.")

elif age < 60:

        print ("You are an adult.")

elif age < 120:

        print ("You are a senior citizen.")

else:

        print ("You have entered an invalid age.")
```

Note that the if...elif structure of decision making is equivalent to a series of nested if...else statements, except more elegant and easier to work with.

Nested If statements

When you begin creating even more complex programs in Python, you may find it necessary to place any of the three if decision making structures inside another if structure to form a structure of nested if statements.

Because nesting if statements can form a complex, even confusing structure, you will need to pay close attention to indentation to differentiate the levels of each if statement. The syntax of this type of conditional statement would take a structure like this:

```
if <condition1>:

    statement(s)

    if <condition2>:

        statement(s)

    elif <condition3>

        statement(s)

    else:

        statement(s)

elif <condition4>:

    statement(s)

else:

    statement(s)
```

Ex.34

```
x = int(input("Enter a positive number x: "))
```

```
y = int(input("Enter a positive number y: "))


if x >= 0 and y >= 0:

        if x > y:

                print ("x is greater than y.")

        elif x==y:

                print ("x and y are equal.")

        else:

                print ("y is greater than x.")

else:

        print ("Either or both x and y are not positive integers.")
```

Here is a good example of a simple nested if statement. Can you identify which if statement is inside the other?

Loops in Python

Loops or loop statements are used to iterate one or more statements multiple times. Python offers three mechanisms for repeatedly executing one or more blocks of code either for a defined number of times or continuously until a defined condition is met.

The three types of loops we will cover in this section are: the **for loop**, the **while loop**, and the **nested loop**.

The for loop

The **for loop** is the most popular loop structure in Python used to iterate over a sequence such as a list, string, tuple, or range (this is discussed further at the end of the chapter). The for loop takes the following general form:

```
for var_name in sequence:

    statement
```

In the syntax above, **var_name** is the variable that assumes the value of the item inside the sequence in every round of iteration. The loop will continue until the last item in the sequence is reached.

The flowchart diagram below simplifies how the for loop works:

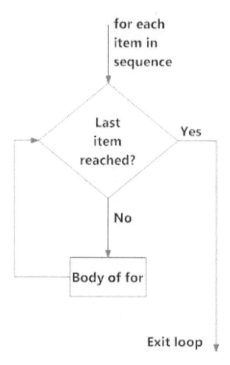

Ex.35

```
for x in range(0,10):

        print("x = ", x)
```

In this exercise, we use the for statement to print the incremental value of x in the range 0 to 10.

The while loop

The while loop is used to iterate over a block of code as long as a test condition returns *True*. The while loop is used when you do not know the number of times to iterate in advance. The syntax of the while loop takes this form:

```
while <condition>:

        statements
```

With the while loop, the test condition is checked first and the body executed only if the test condition evaluates to *True*. This type of loop checks the test condition after each cycle of iteration until the test condition evaluates to *False*. The figure below is a flowchart diagram of the while loop:

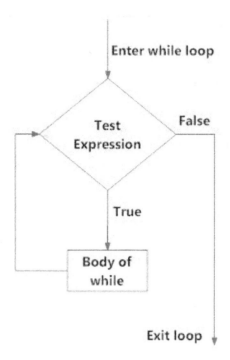

Ex.36

```
total = 0



x = 1

xmax=eval(input("Enter the maximum integer for total: "))

while x <= xmax:

        total+= x

        print (total)

        x+=1
```

```
print ("The total is", total)
```

In this example, the value of variable x increases from 1 to the value entered by the user assigned variable name **xmax**. Note that because the range command is not used in this iteration, **xmax** is used directly as a parameter in the loop.

In Ex37, we use the while loop to iterate a string a number of times the user specifies.

Ex.37

```
my_text = input("Enter a word to iterate: ")

loops = int(input("Enter times to iterate: "))


x = 1


while x <= loops:

        print (my_text, "X", x)

        x = x+1
```

Nested loop

Just the way we put an if statement inside another to create a nested if structure, we can also put a loop a while or for loop inside another loop. The rules and structure for a nested loop in Python is pretty much the same as the rules of nested if.

An important note about nesting loops is that you can put any type of loop inside any other type of loop. This means a for loop can fit inside another for loop or while loop and vice versa. The syntax of a basic nested loop would look like any of these:

```
for var in sequence:

for var in sequence

    statements

statement
```

```
for var in sequence:

while <condition>:

    statements

statementsr
```

```
while <condition>:

for var in sequence:

    statements

statements
```

```
while <condition>:

While <condition>:
```

```
    statements

statements
```

Study Ex38, which finds and prints prime numbers between 2 and 100, to understand how a nested loop is structured.

Ex38

```
x = 2


while (x < 100):

        y = 2

            while (y <= (x/y)):

                    if not(x%y):

                            break

                y = y + 1

            if (y > x/y):

                    print (x, " is a prime number.")


        x = x + 1


print ("Maximum number 100 reached.")
```

Loop control statements

In the previous section, we learned that loops iterate over a block of code until a certain condition is met, or until the test condition returns False. However, sometimes, you may wish your program to terminate an ongoing iteration or an entire loop without necessarily checking the test condition. In such a case, you use a loop control statement.

Loop control statements are used to alter the normal flow of a looped block of code. Python supports three control statements: **break**, **continue**, and **pass**.

The break statement

The break statement terminates the loop it is contained in and transfers the flow of execution to the statement immediately following the body of the loop. If the break statement is contained inside a nested loop, its use will cause the innermost loop to terminate.

The syntax for the break statement is simply **break**.

Ex39

```
for letter in "Success":

        print ("Current letter:", letter)

        if letter == "e":

                break

print ("Found letter:", letter)
```

In this example, the interpreter iterates through the letters in the word "Success" until it finds letter "e", after which it breaks the cycle and the program flow is transferred to the last line outside the loop.

The continue statement

Unlike break, the continue statement does not terminate the loop and instead breaks the current loop and skips the remaining loop statements. It then moves control back to the beginning of the loop to retest the condition and resume iteration.

The syntax for this loop control is **continue**.

Ex40

```
for letter in "Success":

        if letter == "e":

                continue

        print ("Current letter:", letter)
```

Ex40 is a lot like Example39, except that we use continue instead of break. Can you explain the effect this change has on the output of the script?

The pass statement

In Python, the **pass** statement is a null statement such that nothing happens when it is executed (a state called NOP or no operation). It is used as a placeholder where a statement is required syntactically but there is no code or command to execute.

Pass is used as a placeholder for a future function or loop that has not been implemented yet. Note, however, that unlike a comment that is completely ignored, the pass statement is not ignored by the interpreter.

Using else: with loops in Python

The else statement that we used in decision making structure if can also be optionally used with both the for and while loops. Just like with the if statement, loops can have the else: block that is executed when test conditions return a **False**.

The syntax for the for and while loop with else: would look like these:

```
for var_name in sequence:

        statement

else:

        statement
```

```
while <condition>:

        statement

else:

        statement
```

The range command

In the examples we used in this chapter, we ask the interpreter to loop over a specified range of integers or characters. The range command is used with the *for* loop to iterate the loop a fixed number of times. There are three ways to use the range command:

range(i): This generates a sequence of integers that begin at 0 and end at *i-1* (not i), increasing by 1 with each iteration.

range(i, j): This command generates a sequence of integers starting at *i* and ending at *i-j*, increasing by 1 with each iteration.

range(i,j,k): This range command generates a sequence of integers that start at *i* and end at *j-1*, increasing by *k* with each iteration.

Chapter 8: Functions and function arguments

When you create a block of code that carries out a specific calculation or an action, a useful way to refer to it is a function. In Python, you will be able to call one instance of code many times and reuse it to avoid having to write similar code over and over in one or more programs you create.

A function takes some input, referred to as input parameters or arguments, and do something with it. It may or may not return a result (value) depending on what you wrote it for. Consider it a way to break down a complex program into modular or smaller chunks for better organization and manageability.

Predefined functions such as *sqrt()* and *cos()* are good examples of in-built functions that come with Python. You can also define your own functions. This is what we will learn in this chapter.

Defining a function in Python

A function is defined using the keyword *def* and assigning it a name. Its syntax takes the following format:

```
def function_name(arguments):

        """docstring"""

        statement(s)
```

The keyword *def* marks the beginning of the function header followed by the function name, a unique identifier that must follow the standard rules of writing identifiers in Python. The arguments section in parentheses is where the optional values or parameters are passed to the function . Note that the end of the function header is marked by a colon (:).

The optional documentation string (docstring) describes what the function does. The statements that make up the body of the function are entered below the docstring and must be indented at the same level, typically one tab or four spaces.

The return statement at the very end of the function exits the function back to the last position from where it was called. Note that return may contain an expression or expressions that get evaluated and a value returned.

Ex41

```
def ODDorEVEN(x):

    """This is a function to determine

    whether a number is even or odd"""

    if (x%2 == 0):

        print (x, "is an even number.")

    else:

        print (x, "is an odd number.")

    return
```

Calling a function

Once you define a function, you can call it from the Python prompt, program, or another function by simply typing its name with appropriate parameters.

To call the ODDorEVEN function we defined in Example41 and test a number (10) whether it is even or odd, you can enter this command on the shell:

```
>>> ODDorEVEN(10)
```

Ex42

```
def ODDorEVEN(x):

        """This is a function to determine

        whether a number is even or odd"""

        if (x%2 == 0):

                print (x, "is an even number.")

        else:

                print (x, "is an odd number.")

        return


x = eval(input("Enter a number to evaluate: "))


ODDorEVEN(x)
```

In this example, we have used the **ODDorEVEN** function from the previous example to demonstrate how to call a function with one argument.

Function arguments

You learned in the previous section how you can define your own function and how to call it. Our **ODDorEVEN** function in Example41 and Example42 takes one argument or value (x). If the function is run without the argument it expects, the interpreter will return an error. Try it. The same will happen if you provide two arguments when the function needs only one.

Therefore, by default, function arguments are required, and they must be passed to the function in the correct positional order.

However, Python offers multiple options for passing arguments of functions including:

1. Positional arguments

Compared to many other languages, Python handles function arguments in a very flexible manner. We already saw in the previous two examples that arguments are assigned values in the format "parameter=value" using the assignment operator. With positional arguments, the values are assigned to function parameters in order of their location. Consider the example below:

Ex43

```
def user_details(age, sex, location):

        """"Practicing positional arguments

        in Python."""


        print ("User is", age, "year old", sex, "from", location)

        return


user_details (21, "male", "Nairobi")

user_details ("male", "Nairobi", 21)
```

In the last two lines of the example above, the interpreter assigns the three supplied parameters to the *user_details* function parameters age, sex, and location in that order. Supplying the argument values in incorrect order causes the function parameters to be assigned incorrect argument values as in the last line.

2. Optional or defaulted arguments

You can provide default values to arguments that a function needs to run using the assignment operator (=). Ex44 demonstrates how to achieve this:

Ex44

```
def greeting (name, timeofday = "morning"):

        """This function generates a user greeting

        including the user name. The user can enter

        the time of day."""


        print ("Good" + timeofday, name + "!")


        return


greeting (name = "Arthur", timeofday = "afternoon")

greeting (name = "Moses")

greeting (name = "Hawk", timeofday = "night")
```

In our example above, the function greeting requires two arguments for parameters *name* and *timeofday*. However, we have set the default value for the *timeofday* parameter as *"morning"*. You can see in the second execution of the function that when the value for *timeofday* is not provided, the default value was used. Because of this, our example does not encounter an error when only the required argument is provided.

Assigning a function argument a default value is also the most practical way of making an argument an optional argument.

3. Keyword arguments

Positional arguments cause a lot of confusion but you can avoid all that by specifying the arguments of a function by their corresponding parameter names even if they are in a different order in the function definition header. When the function arguments have defined parameters, you can assign argument values without worrying about their positions.

Ex45

```
def user_details(age, sex, location):

    """More about keyword arguments

    in Python"""

    print ("User is", age, "year old", sex, "from", location)

    return


user_details (location = "New York", age = 32, sex = "female")

user_details (sex = "male", location = "Nairobi", age = 21)
```

You can see in the above example that this approach even lets you mix positional and keyword arguments. However, note that if your function has both positional and keyword arguments, you will need to arrange the positional arguments in their order first.

4. Arbitrary number of arguments

We have established that keyword arguments allow a lot of flexibility especially when calling the function. It allows you to create a function that can handle numerous situations including when reused in other scripts. However, no matter what order you supply the required arguments, you must provide a fixed number of arguments as specified in the function.

With Python, you can create a function that accepts a sequence of arbitrary arguments by placing an asterisk in front of the argument.

Ex46

```
def user_details(name, age, *comments):

        """Assigning an arbitrary number of arguments

        to a function"""

        print ("User name:", name, "| Age:", age, "| Comments:",
comments)


user_details("Mariah", 25, "Website: mariah.com")

user_details("James", 30, "Plays basketball", "email: james@email.com")

user_details(name = "Mr. King", age = 50)
```

In this demonstration, by placing an asterisk (*) before the ***comments*** parameter, we have enabled it to take any extra arguments passed to the function. The second to last line of the script calls the function and supplies four arguments when only three are defined in the function header but the program runs without an error. Can you find out how many more arguments you can add?

5. Arbitrary number of keyword arguments

Besides enabling your functions to accept an arbitrary number of undefined arguments, you can also create functions in Python that accept an arbitrary number of keyword arguments.

Ex47

```
def products(prod_name, price, **kwargs):

    """Assigning an arbitrary number of keyword arguments

    to a function"""


    print ("Product name:", prod_name, "| Price:", price)

    print ("Description:", kwargs)


products("Cup", "$10", color = "Red", manufacturer = "ABC co.")

products("Plate", "$5", material = "China ceramic", size = "Family size")

products("Cuttlery", "$25", set_no = "P87439", spoons = 12, forks = 12, knives = 2)
```

As you can see in this example, adding *kwargs* means that an arbitrary number of other parameter=value pairs can be added during run time.

Chapter 9: File Operations

You have learned a lot so far, but all the examples we have been using either have static data (the data types that we typed into the script for demonstration) or can take temporary user input that is lost when we exit the shell. Practical programming involves working with files to read and store permanent data for the program scripts. This is what you will be introduced to in this chapter.

A computer file can be defined as a named storage location on a volatile memory device, such as the hard disk, where data is recorded to be accessed and/or modified later. File operations or file handling in Python is a three-step process that includes:

1.   Open a file object.
2.   Using the file object to read and write data.
3.   Closing the file object.

Before we proceed, we need a file to work with in this chapter. Use a text editor application on your computer to create a text file called *days.txt* with a list of the days of the week in a directory you can access with ease such as the desktop or the location of the Example files.

Opening a file

A file must be opened before it can be read or written into. Python comes with the inbuilt *open()* function that returns the file object or handle that is used to read and write the file. The syntax for opening a file is:

```
file object = open(file_name, [access_mode], [buffering], [encoding])
```

File object: Using the open() function creates a file object that is used to call other associated methods.

file_name: This is a string argument that contains the name of the file you want to open.

access_mode: Access mode is an optional parameter that determines how the file will be accessed or manipulated. The table below presents the list of access_mode argument values and what they mean:

Mode	Mode description
r	This is the default mode. Opens the file for reading only and places the file pointer at the beginning of the file.
rb	Opens the file in binary format for reading only with the pointer placed at the beginning of the file. This is the default mode when the file is opened in binary.
r+	Opens the file for reading and writing with the pointer placed at the beginning of the file.
rb+	Opens the file in binary format for reading and writing with the pointer placed at the beginning of the file.
w	Opens the file for writing only. It creates a new file if it does not already exists or overwrites it if it already exists.
wb	Opens the file in binary format for writing only. If the file exists, it is overwritten and if it does not then new one is created.

w+	Opens the file for reading and writing. If the files exists, it is overwritten and if it does not then a new one is created for reading and writing.
wb+	Opens the file in binary format for reading and writing. If the files exists, it is overwritten and if it does not then a new one is created for reading and writing.
a	Opens the file for appending with the file pointer at the end of the file. If the file does not exist, a new one is created for writing.
ab	Opens the file in binary for appending with the file pointer at the end of the file. If the file does not exist, a new one is created for writing.
a+	Opens the file for both reading and appending. If the file exists it is opened in append mode with the pointer placed at the end of the file if it does not a new one is created for reading and writing.
ab+	Opens the file in binary format for both reading and appending. If the file exists it is opened in append mode with the pointer placed at the end of the file if it does not a new one is created for reading and writing.

Table 18: Descriptions of file open() access modes in Python

[buffering]: If a value of 1 is set, the interpreter will buffer lines while accessing the file. If the value is greater than 1, buffering will depend on the buffer size. When the value is set to 0 or a negative number, the default action which is no buffering will run.

[encoding]: This option is included in this list but it only applies to text files. Different operating systems use different encoding standards for text files. For instance, Linux uses "utf-8" while Windows uses "cp1252". It is a good programming practice to specify the type of encoding when manipulating text files.

Let us try to open our file, days.txt:

Ex48

```
my_text = open ("/home/Computer/Python36-21/Examples/days.txt")
```

Remember to replace the path on Ex48 with the path to your text file.

Reading from a file

To read the content of a file, you must open it in reading mode first and assign the object created to a variable. Python offers three ways to read the data stored in in the file:

Using the <file>.read() method

This method returns all the content of the file as a single string. To view the content of our days.txt file using this method, we would write the code as follows:

```
my_text = open ("/home/Computer/Python36-21/Examples/days.txt")



My_text.read()
```

Using the <file>.readline() method

This method reads the opened file one line at a time and returns the content up to and including the next newline character.

```
my_text = open ("/home/Computer/Python36-21/Examples/days.txt")



My_text.readline()
```

Using <file>.readlines() method

This method returns the list of lines in the file, each item on the list representing one line in the file.

```
my_text = open ("/home/Computer/Python36-21/Examples/days.txt")



My_text.readlines()
```

Writing to a file

A file must be opened in write ('w'), append ('a'), or exclusive creation mode ('x') to be written into. It is important to know that opening the file in write mode ('w') will result in overwriting the contents of the file if it already exists.

The *<file>.write()* method is used to write a string into the file.

Ex49

```
my_text       =       open       ("/home/Computer/Python36-
21/Examples/Seasons.txt")



my_text.write("Seasons of the Year:\n")
```

```
my_text.write("Fall.\n")

my_text.write("Summer.\n")

my_text.write("Spring.\n")

my_text.write("Winter.\n")
```

The script in this example will create a new text file called Seasons.txt if does not already exist.

Closing a file

Your program must properly close a file when the user is done with reading or updating the contents. Closing a file is important because it frees up the memory and processing resources used by the open file. A file is closed using the *close()* method.

Ex50

```
Seasons = open ("path/Seasons.txt")


#File operations


seasons.close()
```

The *close()* method is not entirely safe because if an exception occurs in the process, the code will exit without closing the file. In the later stages of studying or practicing Python, you will be introduced to the try...finally approach.

Python file methods

There are quite a number of methods that come with the Python file object, some of which we have already looked at in this chapter. There are many more that you will encounter when practicing what you have learned here and in the intermediate and advanced stages of studying to program in Python. The table below describes a few of the most common.

Method	Description
flush()	Flushes the write buffer of the file stream.
readable()	Returns **True** if the file stream can be read from.
writable()	Returns **True** if the file stream can be written to.
seekable()	Returns **True** if the file stream supports random access.
tell()	Returns the current file location.
truncate(size=None)	Resizes the file stream to the specified "size" bytes. If "size" is not specified, it resizes to current location.

Table 19: File methods in Python

Chapter 10: Conclusion and Further Reading

That you have reached the last chapter of this book is a testament that you have paid the initial price of becoming a proficient Python programmer. Congratulations!

This coursebook walked you through all the most important topics for a beginner in programming with Python, along with 50 Examples that we hope made it easier to understand what you learned. We hope that in your case, it achieved what we intended.

Python is currently the most popular programming language and millions of newbies and programmers proficient in other languages are taking the time to learn it.

Being a general purpose program, Python is used almost everywhere today - - from front-end game development and back-end web server systems to automotive autonomous systems and home appliances and everything in between. Having Python coding experience under your belt certainly advances your marketability and value in the modern world.

The process of learning the basics of Python must have been daunting, even frustrating, for you, but you have earned the bragging rights of a programmer (or developer, whichever you fancy). We have attempted to make this book easy to understand, practical, and more importantly, fun. However, everything in this book can only take you half the way to proficiency; the rest of the learning process will demand your effort.

Further learning

Now that you have reached the end of the book, what next? We will not abandon you. Here are a few pointers that you will find highly beneficial.

Check out the official Python tutorials

The official Python tutorials on python.org are a goldmine for enthusiastic learners who want a technical and professional explanation of anything to do with the language. Make a point of checking out what it has to offer you.

Make Wikibooks your friends

One of the best sources to learning anything new on the internet is through wikibooks. Wikibooks on Python provide solid, accurate, and concise assistance to learners seeking answers to almost any question without getting too technical.

Online tutorials

Everything you have learned thus far is explained in at least one other tutorial on the internet, albeit with a different approach or examples. Most tutorials feature screenshots or diagrams, and even live online IDLE platforms that enable you to test your code right from the browser. They include the ***Nettuts+'s Python from Scratch*** resource (https://code.tutsplus.com/series/python-from-scratch--net-20566) and Tutorials Point (http://tutorialspoint.com/python3/)

Move on to the next book

Investing in a carefully created book such as this one is by far the most reliable way to learn a topic such as Python programming. Now that you have completed all the basics, perhaps your next step will be to find a book for intermediate to advanced Python learners.

Get all answes at StackOverflow

If you have not created an account at StackOverflow, do so now. This is the one place where millions of developers ask and answer questions to any and every problem you will ever face. Encountered a new error you do not understand? Someone at StackOverflow will explain it to you. Most often you will find someone else already asked your type of question and received the right answer(s).

Practice at Project Euler and CodeFights

With what you know so far, you can barely create a functional application program. The only way to reinforce what you have learned is through practice. Two of the most popular places to flex your coding skills are Project Euler (http://projecteuler.net) and CodeFights (http://codefights.com). Check them out.

Build a Game

Nothing is as satisfying to a budding developer as building his/her own game. The learning curve to developing a playable game may be steep, but it will be very rewarding in the process. You can start using the PyGame (http://www.pygame.org/news) library with one of the thousands of free tutorials to develop a simple Python game to reinforce what you have learned and put it in practical application.

Familiarize yourself with common Python tools and libraries

There is a seemingly endless supply of Python tools and libraries for almost any purpose on the internet. To get you started check out PyPy (http://pypy.org/), NumPy + SciPy (http://numpy.scipy.org), BeautifulSoup (https://www.crummy.com/software/BeautifulSoup/), The Python Image Library (http://www.pythonware.com/products/pil/), and the Django framework (http://djangoproject.com).

Get involved in open source projects

If you believe you have a decent grasp of the Python language and can apply it to real life applications, the best way to learn while doing is by joining open source developers on Github or Bitbucket and contributing to ongoing projects. You will be able to see the approaches other developers use to solve problems and sharpen your coding skills with every line of code you write.

These are just a few of the best places to go to next, now that you are armed with the essential Python coding skills that you must continually build on until you become a pro.

-end-

www.ingramcontent.com/pod-product-compliance
Lightning Source LLC
Chambersburg PA
CBHW070845070326
40690CB00009B/1712